GROWING
Farm, School and Me!

Written and illustrated by sixth-grade students
of Reiffton School in Reading, Pennsylvania

This book is dedicated to Alice and Ronald Herbein
whose farm gave us a place to grow.

It is also dedicated to Dr. Nicholas Corbo
who supervised our growth.
Good luck on your retirement.

I go to school where cows once grazed.

I hear the shrill sound of the whistle being blown
by the referee on the soccer field where
warm conversations once filled the dining room
of the farmhouse.

I step on home plate where Mr. Herbein used to plant
barley, corn, and oats. At the edge of my playground,
I look at many tall, majestic trees that grew with the farm
and will continue to grow with the school.

Ronald Herbein's grandfather purchased the farm
and it was passed to his father and then on to him.
They all lived on the farm working hard all day.
On the farm, there were cows, crops, and a big red tractor.

The rumble of Ronald's cherry-red tractor,
the sweet fragrance of fresh-cut hay, and joyfully wandering
down a dusty dirt path after a long day of school
are some of his fondest memories.

Three generations of hard-working Herbein women baked rich,
luscious chocolate cake to serve after each dinner.
The adults coming in from a long day of farm work
and the children, from a busy day of school, looked forward
to a family dinner followed by a cake, which they washed down
with cold milk.

Where the feed corn once grew, the only thing growing now is the population as the houses go up.

Joseph Herbein, Ronald's father, made the difficult decision
to sell the farm. He preferred his farmland to become a school instead of houses.
His wish was granted.

But along with the farm, the animals had to go, too.
They auctioned off absolutely everything from cows to tractors,
but the one thing they didn't sell were the memories.

Dr. Corbo, the superintendent of my school,
is now in charge of the land. He says there
will be more schools built because of the large,
growing population.

PROPOSED ELEMENTARY
SCHOOL

The design of this school is a daily reminder that this was once a farm. As you enter the school, the architects placed a large hex sign, a sun wheel, on the floor. The cherry wood doors are meant to resemble stalls. Featured on the outside of my school are eye-catching tiles of cows, chickens, and hex signs designed, created, and installed by the students. The tiles glisten on beautiful sunny days.

And on a windy day at my school, there is a cow weather vane that moves with the blowing wind. Also featured on the building façade is a large, barn-red metal hex-sign sculpture surrounded by small cows. All of the silent cows remind us of the live cows that once roamed the Herbein Farm.

Which brings me to Farm Day....

On May 6, my school held Pennsylvania German Farm Day.
At the event there was ice cream, a red tractor, and an enormous
black-and-white cow. There was dancing, singing, and craft making.
One of the most visited workshops was the history of the Pennsylvania Dutch.
Pennsylvania German Day brought together the school and community.

As we honored our past, I look forward to the future.

remembering...

Herbein
FARM

Mr. Herbein loved to work. He told me that working is a wonderful thing. He told me to keep on working and never to give up. If I do those things, he said I would become a better student. As the crops grew with Mr. Herbein, I grow on the same land with my teachers.

Dr. Corbo, the superintendent of the Exeter Township School District, gave me some advice on how to be a better student, too. There's always something to learn every day. Do the best you can do, and always think you can do a little better. *"Be the BEST student you can be!"*

Meet the Authors and Illustrators

In alphabetical order:

Nick Ambrosi
Kayla Arantowicz
Alison Boettlin
Sophia Bonifante
Mary Carpenter
Alexandra Fisher
Megan Jones
Allyssa Krick
Chris Landis
Katie Murphy
Bryn O'Reilly
Katelyn Reifsnyder
Morgan Sandritter
Bristol Sauer
Laura Smith
Bridget Strawn
Aliki Torrence
Maggie Wallner

Project Coordinators
Timothy Dewalt, Art Specialist; David Myers, Reading Specialist; Mimi Shapiro, Artist In Residence;
Gail Torrence, Parent; Sheila Violand, ESL, Instructional Support Teacher

Kids Are Authors®
Books written by children for children

The Kids Are Authors® Competition was established in 1986 to encourage children to read and to become involved
in the creative process of writing.

Since then, thousands of children have written and illustrated books as participants in the Kids Are Authors® Competition.

The winning books in the annual competition are published by Scholastic Inc.
and are distributed by Scholastic Book Fairs throughout the United States.

For more information:
Kids Are Authors® 1080 Greenwood Blvd.; Lake Mary, FL 32746
Or visit our web site at: www.scholastic.com/kidsareauthors

ISBN 10: 0-545-04882-6

ISBN 13: 978-0-545-04882-8

12 11 10 9 8 7 6 5 4 3 2

Cover and Book Design by Bill Henderson

Printed and bound in the U.S.A.   First Printing, June 2007